st Century Skills INNOVATION LIBRARY

LittleBits

CHERRY LAKE PUBLISHING • ANN ARBOR, MICHIGAN

by Amber Lovett

CHERRY LAKE
Publishing

A Note to Adults: Please review the instructions for the activities in this book before allowing children to do them. Be sure to help them with any activities you do not think they can safely complete on their own.

A Note to Kids: Be sure to ask an adult for help with these activities when you need it. Always put your safety first!

Published in the United States of America by Cherry Lake Publishing
Ann Arbor, Michigan
www.cherrylakepublishing.com

Series Editor: Kristin Fontichiaro
Photo Credits: Cover and page 1, ©Ultra-lab/tinyurl.com/j5aqplb/CC BY-SA 2.0; page 4, ©Kevin Jarrett/tinyurl.com/zwrzdva/CC BY 2.0; pages 5, 7, 8, 11, 13, 14, 15, 16, 18, 20, 23, 26, and 27, Amber Lovett; page 9, ©Ultra-lab/tinyurl.com/jodj3bs/CC BY-SA 2.0; page 25, ©Will/tinyurl.com/ hb8mpnb/CC BY 2.0; page 28, ©Ultra-lab/tinyurl.com/hajjanj/CC BY-SA 2.0

Library of Congress Cataloging-in-Publication Data
Names: Lovett, Amber, author.
Title: Littlebits / by Amber Lovett.
Other titles: 21st century skills innovation library. Makers as innovators.
Description: Ann Arbor, Michigan : Cherry Lake Publishing, [2016] |
   Series: 21st Century Skills Innovation Library. Makers as innovators |
   Audience: Grades 4 to 6.- | Includes bibliographical references and index.
Identifiers: LCCN 2016000452| ISBN 9781634714150 [lib. bdg.] |
   ISBN 9781634714310 [pbk.] | ISBN 9781634714235 [pdf] |
   ISBN 9781634714396 [ebook]
Subjects: LCSH: Electronics—Juvenile literature. | Electronic
   systems—Juvenile literature. | Inventions—Juvenile literature.
Classification: LCC TK7820 .L68 2016 | DDC 621.381—dc23
LC record available at http://lccn.loc.gov/2016000452

Cherry Lake Publishing would like to acknowledge the work of The Partnership for 21st Century Learning. Please visit www.p21.org for more information.

Printed in the United States of America
Corporate Graphics
July 2016

Contents

Chapter 1

What Are LittleBits?

How many electronic items have you used today? When you woke up this morning, you might have brushed your teeth with an electric toothbrush. Maybe you used a hair dryer after your shower. Or a printer to print out a homework assignment. Did you turn on a TV today? How about a phone, tablet, or computer?

At take-apart workshops (also known as wreck labs or appliance autopsies), you get to take apart unused machines and discover the electronic circuits inside. Make sure you ask an adult before taking anything apart.

With LittleBits, you can build your own electronics.

Chances are good that you have spent a lot of time today using electronics. Researchers say that the average American spends over 11 hours every day using smartphones, listening to the radio, watching TV or movies, playing video games, or using a computer. Yet many of us do not know how these items actually work.

It is often hard to open up electronic devices to examine their parts and see how they work. It can even be dangerous! You might hurt yourself or break something. Luckily, you can use LittleBits instead!

Inventor Ayah Bdeir created LittleBits as a way to encourage people to become more familiar with how electronics work. She also hoped that her creation might inspire users to invent new devices of their own.

One of the most important ways that inventors create things is through experimentation. Experimenting means testing out different things to see what happens.

The Magic Is in the Magnets

One of the things that makes LittleBits special is that they connect to each other using magnets. When the bits snap together, energy can flow from one piece to the next through wires inside each piece. This is how all electronics work. But instead of using magnets, regular electronic parts are usually connected by **soldering** or **welding**. Solder is a type of metal that melts at a lower temperature than other metals. This melted metal is used like glue. When it cools, it hardens and holds pieces of metal together.

Welding connects two metal pieces by melting each piece, joining them, and letting them harden together. Welding is stronger than solder. However, it is more difficult and requires special training to do. Both soldering and welding also need special tools. LittleBits can be snapped together and broken apart without any tools at all!

LittleBits are great for experimenting because they are **modules**. That means you can easily attach or separate each building block, or bit. You can build new things by using the same pieces over and over. This might remind you of another popular toy: Lego bricks. When Bdeir created LittleBits, she was inspired by how every Lego brick can be attached to any other. With enough bricks, you can create any kind

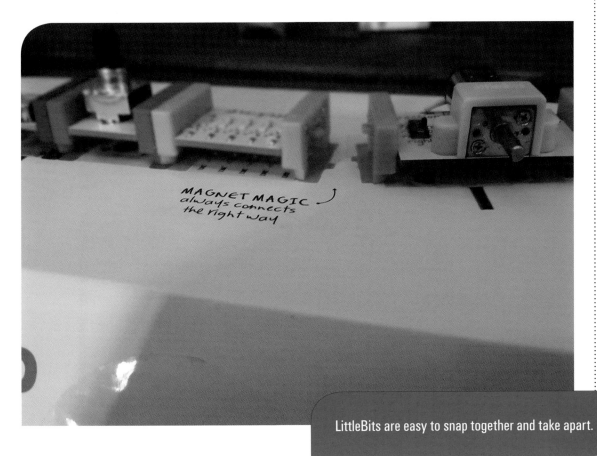

MAGNET MAGIC
always connects
the right way

LittleBits are easy to snap together and take apart.

of building you can dream of. Bdeir wanted to make something similar with electronic parts. After plenty of experimentation, she came up with a design for electronic "bricks" that work together in many different ways.

Each LittleBits piece has a specific function. Some pieces supply power by connecting to a battery,

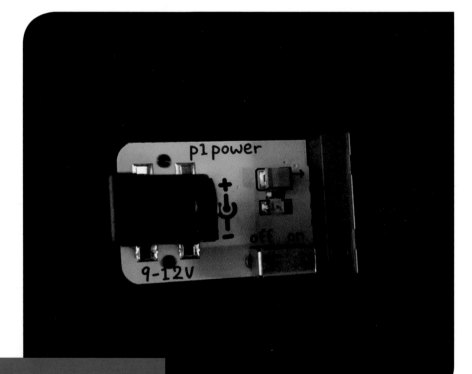

You can plug batteries and other power sources into power bits. This power bit is about the size of a postage stamp.

The LittleBits Base Kit contains everything you need to get started.

computer, or outlet. Others wait for some kind of action or signal, called an **input**. Wire bits act just like a regular wire by connecting different pieces together. This allows you to add different branches to your project. The last kind of bits are **output** bits. Output bits can seem like the most exciting bits, because they are the ones that actually do something. However, output bits depend on the other types of bits to function. You'll learn more about each of these types of bits in the next chapter.

So how do the different kinds of LittleBits connect to each other? Magnets! Magnets have two poles: north and south. Opposite poles attract each other. However, two north or two south poles push against each other and will not connect no matter how hard you try. This ensures that the bits always fit together correctly. You can't make a mistake connecting two LittleBits pieces. If you try to connect two bits upside down or backward, the magnets inside each piece will repel each other. When the pieces are positioned correctly, they will snap together. Simply give them a little tug to separate them again.

You may already have a LittleBits kit. You might also use one at school. Or you may be thinking about purchasing one. There are many different kits you can purchase. The Base Kit is a good option for beginners. There are also special kits. The Synth Kit helps you create music. The Space Kit lets you build your own Mars Rover. One of the great things about LittleBits is that the parts from different kits all work together. So, if you decide to purchase a different kit later, you can combine the pieces to create even more projects.

Chapter 2

How LittleBits Work

Connecting LittleBits together forms a **circuit**. Circuits are the basis of most electronics you use every day. Circuits work by moving electricity through wires. The electricity moves from the source of the power through the wire to the output. The word *circuit* sounds like *circle* for a reason.

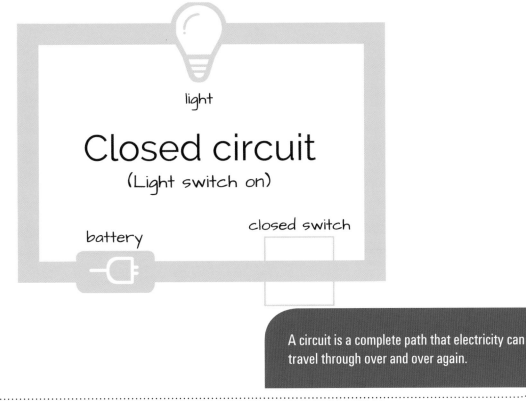

light

Closed circuit
(Light switch on)

closed switch

battery

A circuit is a complete path that electricity can travel through over and over again.

"Hello World"

Whenever you are testing a new output, you can check to make sure it works by connecting it directly to the power. Computer programmers do this when testing out new code. This is called a "Hello World" program. It's useful because it helps them make sure that everything is working properly before they begin diving deeper into a project. Try it now with your bright LED bit. Connect the LED to the blue power bit. Make sure the power bit is connected to a battery and the switch is turned on. When the power bit is on, the LED should light up!

Anything that blocks the flow of the electricity will disrupt the circuit, like a break in a circle. When this happens, the power cannot reach the output.

Often, circuits have **switches** that let you control the flow of power. Think of a light switch. When the switch is in the off position, the circuit is not complete. The electricity cannot flow to the lights. When you change the switch to the on position, the circuit is completed. The electricity can flow to the lights, turning them on. LittleBits power bits have on and off switches, too. They work just like a light switch by allowing the energy from the power source to flow to the next piece.

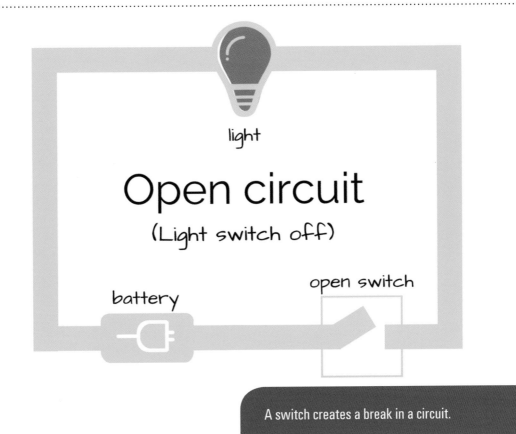

light

Open circuit

(Light switch off)

open switch

battery

A switch creates a break in a circuit.

Everything you make with LittleBits needs at least two bits: a power bit and an output bit. Power bits are blue. They are the first bits you will use in any of your projects. Without a power bit, the rest of your pieces will not have the energy to do what they are supposed to do. This is just like how a lamp will not turn on if it is unplugged. To use a power bit, you must connect it to a power source. Most of the time, you will connect it to a 9-volt battery. Some power bits can also be connected to a power source with a USB port, such as a computer or a phone charger.

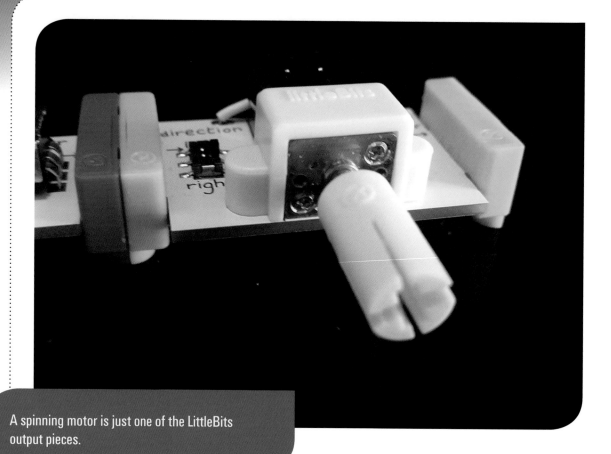

A spinning motor is just one of the LittleBits output pieces.

Power by itself does not actually do anything. It simply moves through the circuit. The parts of electronics that do something are the outputs. In the example of a lamp, the output is the lightbulb. It receives power and turns on when the circuit is complete. LittleBits outputs include a motor that can turn a wheel and a speaker that plays sounds and music. When you begin your project, it is a good idea to first decide which output you want to use. LittleBits outputs are always green.

There are two other kinds of LittleBits that are not required for every project. However, they can be used to create more complex devices. These are inputs and wires. Input bits are pink. They come before an output and change it in some way. A dimmer on a light switch is a good example of an input. How far you turn the knob determines how bright the lights are. If your output is a speaker playing music, an input might change

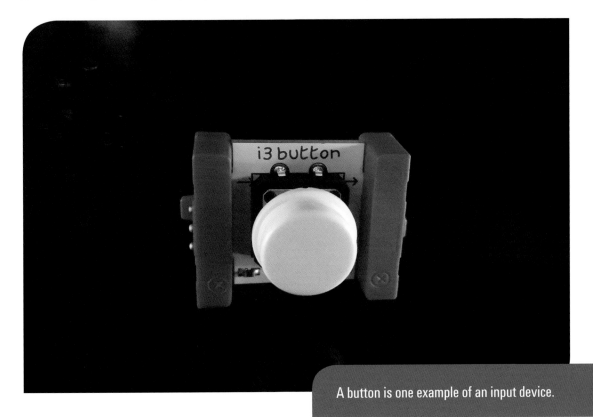

A button is one example of an input device.

how loud the music plays. Other inputs act like a switch by waiting for a specific trigger. A heat sensor input could make your output come on only when it detects a specific temperature. This is how thermostats work to control the temperature of your home. Or perhaps you want a light that turns on automatically when it is dark. You could add a light sensor input between the power and the light output. That's right—you can build your own night-light using LittleBits! Inputs are a

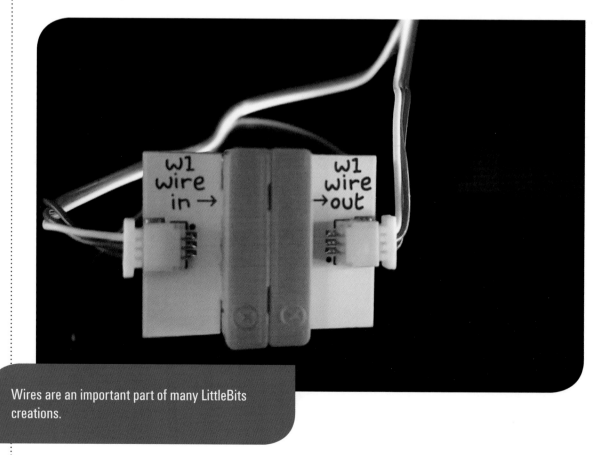

Wires are an important part of many LittleBits creations.

great way to customize your projects and make them work exactly how you want. When you assemble a project, try changing the knobs, switches, and slides on the inputs. Watch how your output changes.

Wire bits are orange. They help you connect your other bits in different ways. Some wire bits have two ends and a long wire in between. These bits are useful if you do not want all your bits to be very close together. You could use a wire bit to put the power and output on separate sides of your project. This might be especially helpful if you are attaching the bits to a large object. Other wire bits can be used to split your project into different branches. These kind of bits have one connector on the first end and two or three on the other. They let you add more inputs and outputs to your project. These inputs and outputs can all operate at the same time. As you become more familiar with LittleBits, you might begin using the wire bits to make more complicated projects. If you use a wire with multiple branches, you have to think carefully about where to put each bit to get the right results. But the great thing is that wire bits let you create unique projects that do exactly what you want them to do!

Chapter 3

Building with LittleBits

N ow that you know more about how LittleBits work, let's try out some projects. The following projects can be done using only the LittleBits Base Kit. Do you have another kit? Try experimenting with different bits and see if you can create your own version!

With LittleBits, you can create a snoop alarm to let you know when someone is looking through your things.

Make It Your Own!

Changing the input you use will change how this project works. If you use the button input instead of the light sensor, you can make an alarm that activates when someone grabs something. If your buzzer is too loud, you can change its volume using the dimmer bit. How else can you change the buzzer? Can you figure out how to turn it into a doorbell for your room?

Project 1: Snoop Alarm

This project shows you how to make a simple alarm. You can place it in a drawer or box to help guard your treasures from thieves (or little brothers and sisters).

You will need:

- P1 power bit
- Battery cord
- 9-volt battery
- Light sensor
- Buzzer

1. Connect the power bit to the battery using the battery cord. The two metal pieces on the flat side of the battery cord should snap into place over the **terminals**. When you switch the power bit on, a red light should turn on. If it doesn't, you may need a new battery.

2. Connect the power bit to your light sensor. The bits should snap together when positioned the right way. Flip the switch on the light sensor to "light." This means the bit will work when it senses light.

3. Add your buzzer after the light sensor. When you turn on your power bit, you should hear the buzzer (unless you are in a dark room).

4. Put your buzzer inside a dark box or drawer. When someone opens it and the light sensor detects light, it will alert you that someone is snooping!

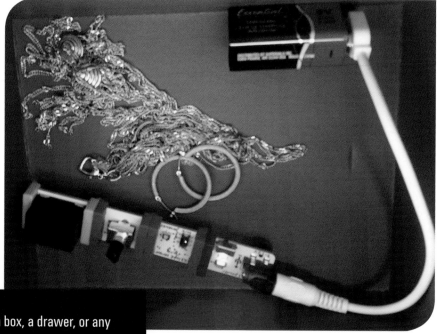

You can put your alarm in a box, a drawer, or any other dark area.

Project 2: Night-Light

Since you have been reading a lot about how circuits work to turn on lights, let's try making a night-light!

You will need:

- P1 power bit
- Battery cord
- 9-volt battery
- Light sensor
- Wire bits
- Bargraph bit
- Small cardboard box
- Scissors
- Tape
- Printer paper

1. Connect the power bit to the battery using the battery cord (see step 1 of project 1 for instructions).

2. Connect the light sensor to the power bit. Now make sure the switch on the light sensor is flipped to "dark." This tells the sensor to turn on the output when it is dark.

3. Add one of the wire bits after the light sensor. Next, add the bargraph bit. Try covering up the light

Customizing Your Night-Light

There are a lot of ways to change the look of your night-light. You can experiment with putting the bits inside a glass or plastic container. Or you could use clear plastic wrap instead of paper. You can create your night-light using any materials as long as they let light through. Each material will change the way the light glows. What will you come up with?

You can also change your project by adjusting the input you use. What will change if you use a dimmer or button instead of the light sensor? Can you create a more complicated project using more than one input? What if you added more than one output? Give it a try and see what happens!

sensor with your hand. The light should turn on when this bit is covered up. Try using one of the purple LittleBits screwdrivers to adjust the sensitivity of the light sensor. Check out how this changes the way the bargraph lights up! That's it—you built a working night-light! Now let's make it look a little nicer.

4. If your cardboard box has flaps, remove them now. You can cut them off with scissors. Next, cut a hole in the back of the box. The hole should be large enough to fit the bits through. Ask an adult if you need help.

5. Disconnect the bargraph from the wire. Pull the end of your wire labeled "Wire in" through the hole in the back of the box.

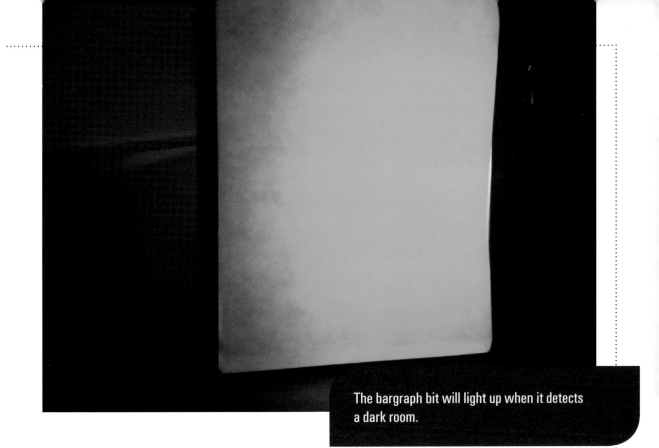

The bargraph bit will light up when it detects a dark room.

6. Reconnect the bargraph inside the box. Tape the bargraph and wire to the inside of the box.

7. Tape the rest of the bits to the back of the box.

8. Wrap a sheet of printer paper around the box and secure it with tape. The paper should cover the box's opening. You might need to trim some edges of the paper, depending on how big the box is. The printer paper will let some light through, but not all. It will make your light look softer.

9. Place your box somewhere dark and watch your night-light glow!

Project 3: Zoetrope

A zoetrope is kind of like a flip book. However, it has a circular shape. And instead of flipping pages, it spins around. The inside of the zoetrope contains a series of drawings. The top has slits the viewer can look through. The slits help to create an illusion that makes it look like the drawings are moving.

You will need:

- A sheet of printer paper
- Scissors
- A recycled circular container, such as a plastic yogurt or cottage cheese container
- Markers
- Tape
- Paint
- Paintbrush
- P1 power bit
- Battery cord
- 9-volt battery
- Dimmer
- DC motor
- Motor mate

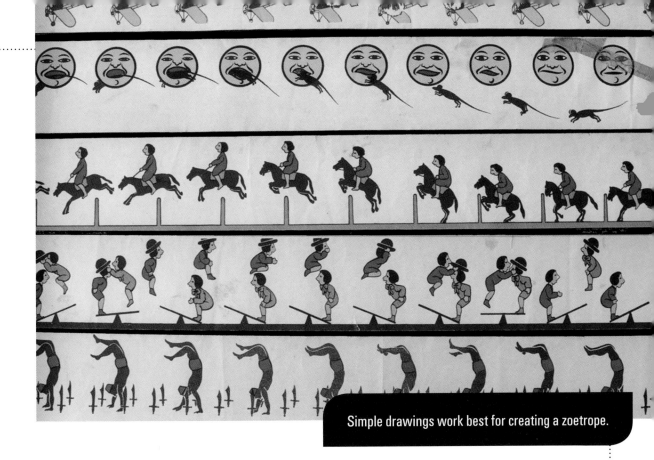

Simple drawings work best for creating a zoetrope.

1. Cut a strip of paper that will fit around the inside of the container.

2. Draw a series of pictures on the strip. Each image in the series should be moved slightly so it looks like movement when you watch them spin. An easy idea to start with is an inchworm crawling. You could also try drawing a person walking or a ball bouncing. Draw anything you think of. Just remember that you will need to draw it over and over again, so something simple and easy to draw is best.

Try to make sure there is equal space between all of the slits on your zoetrope.

3. Line up the strip of drawings along the bottom of the container. Tape it to the inside of the container.

4. Cut slits along the top of the container about every 1 inch (2.5 centimeters) or so. Ask an adult if you need help. The slits should be about 0.5 inches (1.3 cm) wide and 1 inch (2.5 cm) long. If your container is more than 3 inches (7.6 cm) tall, you should cut it to make it shorter. If the slits are too far above the drawings, they will be too hard to see.

5. Paint the outside of your zoetrope. This will help make your animation look even better because you will not be distracted by the pictures on the outside of the container. Let the paint dry completely before continuing on to the next step.

6. Poke a hole through the bottom of the container. The hole should be big enough to fit the motor mate through.

What else do you want to create with your LittleBits kit?

7. Connect the power bit to the battery using the battery cord (see step 1 of project 1 for instructions).

8. Connect the dimmer to the power bit. Then add the DC motor.

9. Slip the motor mate over the D-shaped part of the DC motor.

10. Slide the motor mate through the hole in the bottom of the container.

11. Turn on your project and look through the slits to watch your animation! Use the dimmer to make the zoetrope spin faster or slower. How does the animation change when you change the direction of the motor?

What Will You Invent?

After you try out these projects, you might be wondering what comes next. The answer is up to you! If you are feeling stuck, try thinking about the world around you. Are there problems that you think you can fix? What about improving something that already exists to make it work better? When you start to understand how electronics work, you might begin to see the world in a new light. This is what being an inventor is all about! Instead of just wishing things were different, you can change them. Just remember: Inventing means making mistakes. You do not have to be frustrated when things go wrong. You can use your mistakes to learn something new. They just might inspire you to create a whole new project!

Glossary

circuit (SUR-kit) an uninterrupted path along which electricity can flow

input (IN-put) information or signals that are received by a device

modules (MAH-joolz) parts that can be combined in different ways and are easily taken apart

output (OUT-put) the result or product of a system

soldering (SAH-dur-ing) melting a special type of metal and using it to join two other pieces of metal

switches (SWICH-iz) equipment that can be used to break the path of electricity in a circuit, as well as reconnect it

terminals (TUR-muh-nuhlz) the two connections on a battery that allow electricity to flow through it

welding (WEL-ding) joining two pieces of metal by melting them and pressing them together as they cool

Find Out More

BOOKS

Bdeir, Ayah, and Matt Richardson. *Make: Getting Started with LittleBits*. San Francisco: Maker Media, 2015.

Gilby, Nancy Benovich. *FIRST Robotics*. Ann Arbor, MI: Cherry Lake Publishing, 2016.

Murphy, Maggie. *High-Tech DIY Projects with Microcontrollers*. New York: PowerKids Press, 2015.

O'Neill, Terence, and Josh Williams. *Arduino*. Ann Arbor, MI: Cherry Lake Publishing, 2014.

WEB SITES

Adafruit Blog
https://blog.adafruit.com/tag/LittleBits-projects
Adafruit is a company that sells LittleBits. Its blog hosts some really neat LittleBits project ideas.

Instructables
www.instructables.com
This is another great Web site where people from all over the world can submit their projects. Try searching for LittleBits to find projects that inspire you.

LittleBits
http://LittleBits.cc/projects
Find instructions for lots of projects created with different LittleBits kits. You can search for projects by kit, type of bit, and keywords.

Index

About the Author

Amber Lovett is a graduate of the University of Michigan School of Information, where she worked with maker activities in libraries and schools.